Louis Braille

루이 브라유

Biography Comic
who? ⑪ Louis Braille

개정판 1쇄 인쇄 2014년 3월 5일
개정판 1쇄 발행 2014년 3월 10일

글 강민희
그림 스튜디오 청비
번역 자넷 재완 신
감수 김수희
펴낸이 김선식

책임편집 김선영 **디자인** 박효영
콘텐츠개발팀장 김선영 **콘텐츠개발팀** 박효영, 이유미, 김선민, 조서인
마케팅본부 이상혁

펴낸곳 스튜디오 다산 **출판등록** 2013년 11월 1일 제414-81-37694
주소 경기도 파주시 회동길 37-14 3층
전화 02-702-1724(기획편집) 02-703-1725(마케팅) 02-704-1724(경영관리)
팩스 02-703-2219 **who클럽** cafe.naver.com/dasankids
종이 월드페이퍼(주) | **인쇄** (주)현문 | **제본** 광성문화사

ISBN 979-11-5639-033-6 (14740)

who?
Louis Braille
루이 브라유

글 **강민희** | 그림 **스튜디오 청비** | 번역 **자넷 재완 신** | 감수 **김수희**

Dasan Kid

Louis Braille

Inventor of Braille system, January 4, 1809 ~ January 6, 1852

Louis Braille, who gave the hope of knowledge to the blind, was born on January 4, 1809, in a small town near Paris, France, called Coupvray. Louis liked playing in his father's workshop but when he was three years old, he pierced his left eye while playing with an awl in the workshop. Then when he was four, his right eye became infected and he lost sight in both eyes.

Louis did not despair in his situation but rather adjusted himself to his new life. The village priest, Jacques Palluy, took note of this special boy and began to give him lessons. Then at age seven, he began attending the local school. However, there was no way for him to read the books.

Father Palluy felt sorry for precocious young Louis who was frustrated about not being able to read books. So he found out about the Royal Institute for Blind Youth in Paris and helped him get in. In 1819, ten-year-old Louis left his family for Paris in hopes to be able to read.

Louis was able to learn to read embossed printing and night writing at the Royal Institute and was very excited about it. But his excitement was fleeting and soon turned to disappointment after he realized that there were many problems with these lettering systems.

However Louis didn't get defeated but rather decided to make a writing system for people like himself who couldn't see. After three years of working on it, in 1824, he perfected a raised dot alphabet using six dots which could express the 26 letters of the alphabet.

Unfortunately, Braille was so absorbed in his alphabet research that he failed to take good care of his health, resulting in his worsening health condition. On January 6, 1852, the year he turned forty-three, Braille died from tuberculosis. He was buried initially in his hometown, Coupvray, but then relocated to France's national cemetery, the Pantheon, one hundred years later.

루이 브라유

점자 발명가, 1809년 1월 4일 ~ 1852년 1월 6일

눈먼 사람들에게 지식의 빛을 준 루이 브라유는 1809년 1월 4일, 프랑스 파리 근처의 작은 마을 꾸브레이에서 태어났습니다. 루이는 아버지의 작업장에서 놀기를 좋아했는데, 3살 때 아버지의 작업실에서 송곳을 가지고 놀다가 왼쪽 눈을 찔리는 사고가 일어났습니다. 그리고 4살 때에는 오른쪽 눈까지 감염되어 두 눈이 모두 안 보이게 되었습니다.

루이는 자신의 상황에 절망하지 않고 새로운 생활에 적응해 나갔습니다. 그런 루이를 기특하게 본 마을의 자크 파뤼 신부님은 루이에게 공부를 시키기 시작하였습니다. 그리고 7살 때에는 마을 학교에서 공부를 하게 되었습니다. 하지만 눈이 보이지 않는 루이가 책을 읽을 수 있는 방법은 없었습니다.

자크 파뤼 신부님은 총명한 루이가 공부를 하지 못해 슬퍼하는 것을 보고 루이를 위해 파리의 왕립맹아 학교에 들어가도록 도와주었습니다. 1819년, 10살이 된 루이는 책을 읽을 수 있다는 말에 가족들과 헤어져 파리의 왕립맹아학교에 입학하게 됩니다.

왕립맹아학교에서 루이는 돋을새김 문자와 야간문자를 알게 되고 무척 기뻐했습니다. 하지만 기쁨도 잠시, 루이는 이 문자들이 실제 사용하는데에는 많은 문제점이 있음을 알게 되고 다시 실망합니다.

루이는 여기서 좌절하지 않고 자신이 눈먼 사람들이 사용할 수 있는 글자를 만들기로 결심합니다. 그리고 3년의 노력 끝에 1824년에 드디어 점 여섯 개로 알파벳 26글자를 모두 표시할 수 있는 점자를 만들어 냈습니다.

자신의 몸을 돌보지 않고 점자 연구에만 몰두했던 루이는 점점 건강이 나빠졌습니다. 1852년 1월 6일, 43살이 되던 해 루이는 폐결핵으로 사망하였습니다. 루이는 고향 마을인 꾸브레이에 묻혔다가 100년이 지난 후 프랑스 국립묘지인 팡테옹으로 옮겨져 영원한 휴식을 맞이하였습니다.

이 책을 만든 사람들

글 · 강민희

어린이들에게 도움이 되는 학습 만화를 만들기 위해 노력하는 젊은 작가입니다. 어릴 적 재미있게 읽은 책이 평생의 꿈을 바꿀 수 있다는 사명감으로 더욱 감동적이고 기억에 남을 만한 이야기를 만들기 위해 노력하고 있습니다.

그림 · 스튜디오 청비

어린이들을 위해 새롭고, 재미있고, 즐거운 이야깃거리를 만드는 만화 창작 집단입니다. 세상을 바꾼 인물들의 삶을 통해 어린이들이 희망찬 미래를 만들어가길 바랍니다. 작품으로 『지식 똑똑 경제 리더십 탐구-긍정의 힘』, 『why? 서양 근대 사회의 시작』, 『why? 세계대전과 전후의 세계』 등이 있습니다. 이 책은 이준형 작가님이 그림을 그리셨습니다.

번역 · 자넷 재완 신(Janet Jaywan Shin)

미국 메릴랜드 주에서 태어나고 자랐습니다. 메릴랜드 대학교에서 언어학을 전공하고 UCLA에서 응용언어학 석사 학위를 취득했습니다. 서울대학교 언어교육원에서 전임 강사, 서울대학교 사범대학교 영어교육과에서 초빙교수로 일했습니다. 감수한 책으로 『서울대생한테 비밀 영어과외받기』가 있고 고등학교 영어 교과서 교정 작업에 참여했습니다.

감수 · 김수희

연세대학교에서 역사를 전공했습니다. 이후 한국뿐 아니라 일본, 미국에서 한국어, 일본어, 영어를 가르쳐 왔으며 부모를 위한 영어교육용 책을 썼습니다. 영어교육채널 EBSe '엄마표 영어특강'에서 강의를 하며 홈스쿨, 알파벳과 파닉스, 다차원 테마 영어 수업 기법을 알리고 있습니다. 전국 각지에서 어린이 영어 교육에 대한 강연을 하며 창의적이고 열정적인 교수법으로 영어를 배우고자 하는 어린이와 부모들에게 많은 도움을 주고 있습니다.

Louis Braille

Louis Braille was the first person to invent the raised dot system of reading and writing for the
_____.

a. old
b. blind
c. sick

Answer: b

Contents

01 A Fateful Accident

CD1 Track 01 ▶

Louis Braille was born on January 4, 1809, in Coupvray, a small town in France.

Louis' father made leather horse saddles for a living. Louis liked watching his father at work.

I'm gonna be a great craftsman like Papa!

No, Louis! This is dangerous!

Why?

You could hurt yourself very badly. You mustn't touch these tools without my permission.

Yes, Papa.

There were many sharp tools that were dangerous for young Louis to play with in his father's workshop.

Why don't you play with this?

OK.

Where are you going, Mama?

I'm going to the market to buy things for supper. Why aren't you playing with Papa in his workshop today?

He went to another village to make a delivery.

Aha, that's why my little Louis looks so down.

Then do you want to go to the market with me?

Sure!

13

At that time, blind people were usually homeless and begged for money, or did work that no one else wanted to do.

I feel sorry for blind people.

You must've been pretty shocked today.

Yes. I'm really glad I can see with my eyes.

Simon, are you there?

Who is it?

16

It's Henri Elyssee! Can you come out for a minute?

It's Henri!

Papa will be right back. Don't play with any of the tools, okay?

I won't.

While alone in his father's workshop, Louis looked for something to play with.

Hmm, I'm bored.

It should be okay to just look at the tools.

I'm a big boy now! I'll just be careful.

The leather was slipperier than he expected. The same was true for the awl handle.

It's hard to make a hole because the leather's so slippery.

It looks easy when Papa does it. Hmmm.

Just then, the awl slipped off the leather, splitting into several pieces, and flew up to hit Louis in the eye.

Ahhh!

What was that?

AHHHHHH

Louis?

Louis!

Waaahh!

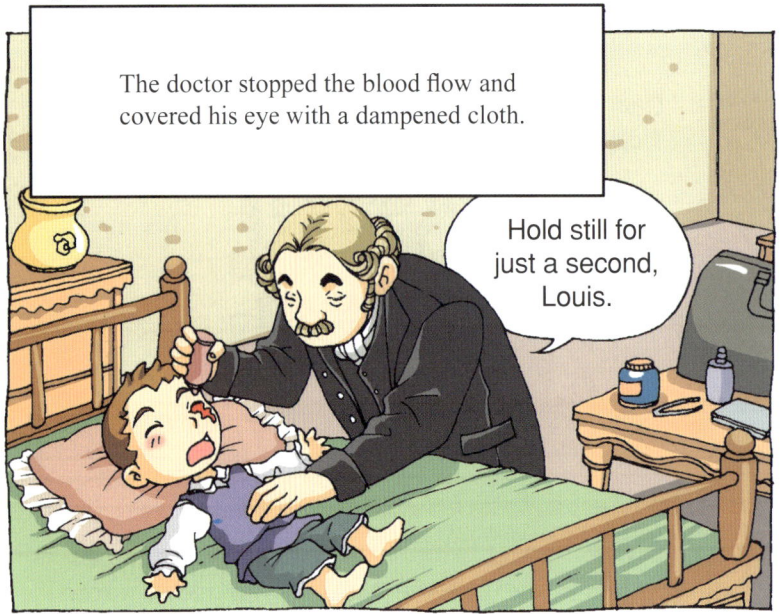

The doctor stopped the blood flow and covered his eye with a dampened cloth.

Hold still for just a second, Louis.

Waah! That hurts!

Let's close the windows and keep the room dark.

There was nothing else, however, that the doctor could do to treat the serious injury.

Despite his parents' diligent care, Louis' condition did not improve at all.

What do you think, doctor?

...

No!

Doctor, please do something!

I'm sorry. There's nothing more I can do.

Louis' injured eye then became infected and as a result, swollen and itchy.

Louis, you're awake. How is your eye?

It doesn't hurt, but it's itchy.

Good, your fever's gone.

You must be hungry. Have some milk.

Huh?

Mama, it looks like there are two cups.

What?

Never mind. It looks like one cup now.

Whew, you scared me.

I wanna go outside and play. I wanna see what Papa's doing, too...

Uh?

Whew, that's better.

Good morning!

That's weird.
It's dark.

I thought it was morning. Is it still night?

24

25

I'm sorry, but there's nothing I can do.

Lo-Louis! My baby!

Louis, left by himself, was still trapped in the darkness surrounding him.

Mama...

Mama, where are you?

What is to become of Louis?

How can he be blind at such a young age? It's impossible.

B-blind? Me?

28

02 Seeing With the Mind's Eye

 Track 11 ▶

Mama, did you bring the candles?

Yes, they're all lit.

No! It's still dark!

Ouch, it's hot!

Honey!

Why is it still dark when all the candles are lit? Why isn't daylight coming?

Sob.

Louis!

I'm so sorry I wasn't there for you when all this happened.

A tear drop...?

Papa's crying. But he's tougher than anyone I know.

I was the one who played with the awl that he said not to touch...

Papa, I'm sorry. You told me not to touch your tools, but I disobeyed you.

No. I shouldn't have left you by yourself.

32

I'm going to bed now.

...

Ow!

Louis, I'll take you to your room.

No! I can go by myself!

How hard it must be for him to suddenly not be able to see everything he used to see.

What can we do?

...

Let's go to a bigger hospital in the city. They'll be able to cure him.

Yes, let's take him first thing tomorrow morning.

Mama, will the new doctor be able to fix my eyes?

Of course.

Then I'll be able to see you and Papa's face again.

That's right. Don't worry.

Louis' parents did everything they could to try to restore his eyesight. They took him to every well-known doctor they had heard about, no matter how far they had to travel.

I'm afraid the cornea* of both eyes has been damaged too severely to be able to recover his sight.

However, they were told each time that there was no hope.

Louis, my dear baby! Don't you worry. We'll take care of you.

I'm sorry.

...

*cornea: A clear membrane through which light enters in the front of the eye.

35

36

As soon as they got home, Louis' father headed straight for his workshop.

This should do the job!

Louis' father began making a cane for his son with the thick tree branch that he brought home.

Wait, is there something here?

TAP

From now on, this is going to be your eye.

Use it to find anything that might be blocking your path.

Aha, it's the sofa! Neat! I can now know if something is in front of me!

Louis, Mama wants you to be a good citizen when you grow up.

I don't want you to have to depend on other people's sympathy and beg for money.

I don't want to be a beggar, either.

So we've decided that even though you can't see, you need to learn how to do things by yourself.

We would like to always be there for you, but that won't always be possible.

It's going to be tough at times but we want you to do your best to learn.

Alright.

It was hard work for a young boy who was blind to try to do things by himself. He tried to become familiar with every part of the house by feeling his way around with his hands.

Ouch!

Oops!

CRASH

As Louis felt his way around, he began to remember where things were, like the dishes and other items on top of the table.

His mother and father silently watched him from a distance. Louis was soon able to move around the house freely without falling or knocking anything over.

Be careful!

Don't worry! We'll guide him.

Louis, if you go a little more, you'll be at the well.

Am I almost there?

Ah, found it!

Think you can find it by yourself?

Yeah, I'll remember!

Good! Then let's pass the vegetable garden and...

Let's go to the church!

Everyone in the family helped to train Louis. None of them wanted him to have a hard life in the future.

From now on, it will be your job to fetch the water for the family. Think you can do it?

No problem!

Is it morning?

The warmth of the sun tells me that it's morning.

Starting today, I'm going to fetch the water by myself.

Aaah!

Louis!

No, even though I want to help him, I need to watch from a distance.

Pshh, I'm not going to cry over this! It doesn't even hurt!

Now where's the bucket?

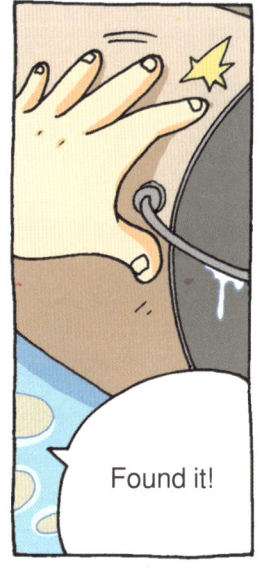

Found it!

I'll just go back and fill the bucket again.

Sometimes, Louis would spill the water on his way back from the well. Whenever he did, he would have to go back to the well and fetch the water again.

Now, let's set the table.

Yes, ma'am!

First get the dishes out and put them on the table.

OK.

Once in a while, Louis would go to his father's workshop and learn how to treat leather.

You have to spread the wax over the leather very carefully.

OK.

All done!

Already?

Wow, this is very well tanned! The shine makes this good quality leather.

While I'm waxing the leather, it quietly whispers to me.

Oh yeah? What does it say?

It says, "All done now." And that's when the tanning* is complete!

Hahaha, that's great!

*tanning: The process of smoothing animal hide in order to make it into soft leather.

45

Louis learned how to see the world not through his eyes, but through his hands, his ears, and his nose.

SWOOSH

GURGLE
GURGLE

CHIRP
CHIRP

But he had a hard time making friends.

It's Louis!

Where?

Uh? I hear my friends' voices. I'd better say hi.

Oh no, he's coming this way.

Let's get out of here! My mom said not to play with Louis.

Why?

…

We could catch the disease that made him go blind!

We could go blind?

Louis liked sitting in front of his house, guessing who was passing by, and greeting them by name.

48

Yes. Every person has a different sound. Madame Renee makes a clickety-clack sound.

And Monsieur Pepe makes a thump-thump sound.

He's quite bright. It's a shame he can't see.

What is your name, sir?

I'm the new priest, Father Palluy.

I'm trying to meet everyone in the village.

My name is Louis. Are you here to visit our house?

Yes.

Come in. I'll show you around.

Thank you.

03 Going to School

Louis is a beggar!
Louis is a beggar!

Ow!

Hey beggar!
Go home!

Stop it!

How did you get hurt like this?

...

What happened?

Mama, why do blind people have to become beggars?

Why can't they get a job?

You need to go to school in order to get a good job.

But blind people can't study.

I see. It's because we can't see the books...

Louis' mother did not know how to reply. She did not know of any way that the blind could study or read on their own.

Mama, I want to study too. There has to be a way.

Well...

How can I be able to study?

Hello there, Louis. Where are you going?

Hello, Father Palluy.

The next day, Louis went to the church. Father Palluy gave him lessons in astronomy, history, and science.

He also told him stories about the good people and bad people in the Bible...

...and about the brave heroes and the fools.

Father Palluy is late today.

I heard Louis Braille is studying with Father Palluy these days.

Right. Apparently, he's quite smart.

But what's the use of being smart when he can't see? Father Palluy seems to be wasting his time.

I agree. That boy's destiny is already determined.

Are they right? Is it pointless for a blind person to study?

No. Father Palluy said that if I study hard, I can become a great person!

I wish he'd come soon. I have to ask him a question.

Louis, I'm sorry for making you wait!

Father, isn't it true that anyone can become a great person if he studies really hard?

Yes, but why do you ask that all of a sudden?

Oh, no reason. Father, you said yesterday that the Earth was round, right?

Yes.

Then why don't the people living on Earth fall off? If the Earth is round like a ball, wouldn't the people living on the bottom fall off?

But that never happens, right?

I saw it here somewhere...

What was it?

55

Actually, the priest did not formally study education. Thus, the more Louis asked difficult questions, the harder it became for him to answer them.

That's it! Let me ask the local school.

I've never taught a blind student before.

I don't have any idea how I would teach him.

Louis is a very intelligent boy. You won't have to do much more for him than you do for the other students.

But no matter how smart he is, when he grows up, he will have no choice but to beg for a living. I'm afraid we'd be giving Louis a false hope.

Sir, Louis has a passion for learning.

And besides, our school has only one classroom. Do you think he'd be able to get along with the other children?

Of course. He's good-natured and cheerful, so he'll be able to make friends easily.

Since you feel that strongly about the child, I will give it a try.

Thank you!

Louis, today will be the last lesson you will have with me.

What? What do you mean?

Did I bother you too much with all of my questions? I won't do it anymore.

Please be my teacher.

Hahaha. It's not that.

Huh?

From now on, you can go to school just like the other children.

I can go to school? I can't believe it!

Papa, what's school like? It's a fun place, isn't it?

Well, some children think it's fun...

...but some don't like to go to school.

They don't like to go? Why? They can learn new things at school. I can't wait to go!

But I'm a little worried for you. Don't you think it would be hard for you to sit all day long at a desk without moving around?

Not at all. If it means I can study, I can sit all day long without moving an inch!

That's right. My Louis is going to do just fine!

You must be Louis. You're new, right?

I'm Monsieur Becheret. I'm going to be your teacher.

I heard a lot about you from Father Palluy. I heard that you're very bright and that you love to study.

58

This is my first time teaching a blind student so I need you to help me, okay?

OK.

We have a new student joining us today. His name is Louis Braille. You might already know this but he's blind. I hope you can all be considerate and get along together.

Yes, sir!

Then we add 12...

Doesn't this class make you sleepy?

Not at all. It's really interesting.

But why don't you pay attention when the teacher asks questions?

Ohhh!

Louis, would you like to answer the next question?

!

Louis?

Yes!

Please pay attention next time.

Yes, sir.

If I could only see this book...

Because he couldn't read the textbook, Louis had to memorize everything the teacher had said in class.

Yawn. Louis, let's go to sleep now.

Can't you just read me a little more? I haven't memorized it all yet.

Young Louis tried to memorize everything he learned in class each day. Sometimes he would study so hard that dawn would come before he knew it.

He studied harder than anyone else. Even though he memorized his lessons, he would continue to meditate on what he had learned.

However, it was hard for Louis to study together with his classmates.

64

The writing must be here.

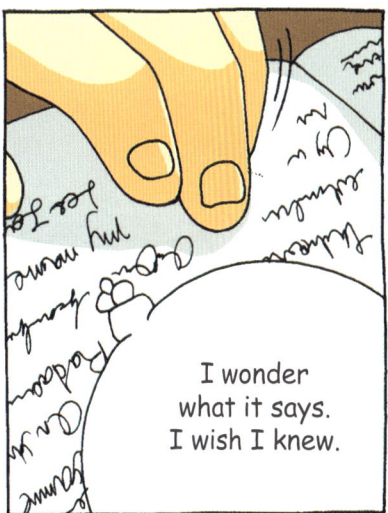

I wonder what it says. I wish I knew.

The more he studied, the more he wanted to be able to read.

Louis, you're staring holes into that book again. Can you actually see something?

No, nothing.

If I could just once be able to read a book, I wouldn't wish for anything else.

Let's talk about this outside.

Sigh, class is already over.

Alright, that's it for today. See you tomorrow.

RING RING RING

Yes, sir! See you tomorrow.

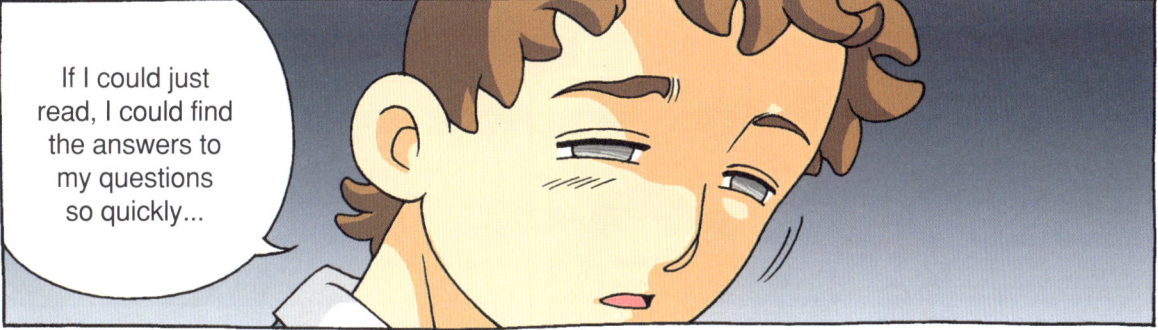

If I could just read, I could find the answers to my questions so quickly...

Why does Louis look so sad?

Louis, did something happen today?

Father, why can't I see? Am I being punished for the bad things I've done?

 **Track 30** ▶

Not at all. What happened to you was purely an accident. Is everything alright at school?

I want to read.

Read?

My friend said that everything I ask about is in the textbook.

I see.

If I could read, then I could learn about why the sun rises and why the sky is blue, couldn't I?

You want to be able to search for the answers yourself.

Yes. I wish I could see for even a day.

That's too bad.

No!

There's no law saying that a blind person cannot become a great person.

Now that Louis is already ten years old, I need to find a good school for him to attend.

If they can teach him how to read and write, that would be even better.

Where can I find a school like that?

04 The Model Student Who Couldn't See

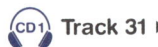

There is a school in Paris called the Royal Institute for Blind Youth. I think it might be a good school for Louis.

He would be able to receive a better quality education there.

We also want Louis to continue learning so that he can have a better future. However, Paris is too far.

Yes, I know.

But this school teaches the children to read using special letters.

Father, did you say letters?

That's right.

You mean that blind people can read and write, too?

I saw for myself students reading books with their fingers.

Louis couldn't hide his excitement at what the priest had just told them. It was like a dream come true for Louis, who thought he could never read for the rest of his life.

Papa, please let me go. I can handle it.

You're too young right now. It would be hard to live in the city by yourself.

No. If it means being able to read, I can face anything!

You know me. If I set my mind to doing something, I'll do it no matter what.

Hmm. Even when he first lost his sight, he would never give up, no matter how many times he fell or got hurt.

Dear, let's send him for the sake of his future.

Yes. I want Louis to have a better life, too.

Yay!

You've made a good decision.

You seem just a teeny bit excited.

Yes! I'll finally be able to read books!

My heart is beating so fast! The books are going to be filled with tons of interesting stuff!

72

Not long afterwards, Louis moved into the dormitory of his new school. As smart and good-natured as he was, however, he was still a young boy who had never been separated from his parents before.

During the day, he was busy looking around the school and meeting new friends. But at the end of the day when he was lying alone in his dorm bed, the sense of loneliness overwhelmed him.

I can't sleep. Whenever I can't sleep, Mama sings me a lullaby.

Mama...

I miss you! Waah!

Don't cry.

W-who are you?

Here, take this.

A... handker- chief?

Everyone goes through a hard time in the beginning. You want to go home and you miss your family, but you'll get used to it here soon.

Really?

I was like that, too. But once you get used to your new life here, you won't feel sad anymore.

My name is Gabriel Gauthier. What's yours?

I'm Louis Braille.

At the Royal Institute for Blind Youth, Louis met Gabriel. Gabriel taught Louis about school life there and would become his lifelong friend.

Nice to meet you, Louis. Welcome to the Royal Institute for Blind Youth.

First let's figure out how many paces it takes to get from your bed to the door.

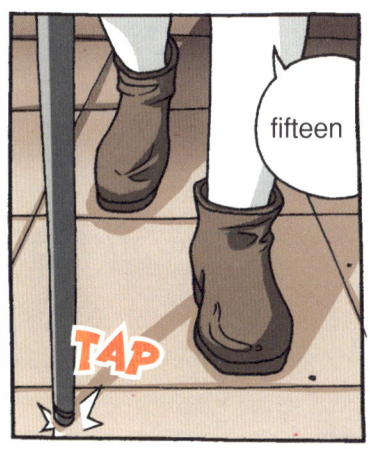

This school's layout is complicated so you have to memorize everything. I still get lost sometimes.

Don't worry. My memory is one thing I can rely on.

Heh heh. Now I'll show you the way and you count the steps as you follow me.

Louis memorized the number of paces between various places, from the dormitory to the stairs, from the stairs to the classroom, cafeteria, and gymnasium.

twenty-seven, twenty-eight...

The school layout was indeed complicated, so Louis would get lost once in a while. But soon he was able to easily find his way around.

Louis received outstanding grades in all his subjects. Not long after he began attending the Royal Institute, he started amazing his teachers and classmates with his high scores.

Would you like to answer this question, Louis?

The answer is 37.

Correct. I only taught you this once, but you caught on quickly. You're a bright boy!

The students learned how to knit hats and gloves, and make slippers out of leather.

Since Louis grew up helping his father make leather, his skills at making things were excellent.

How is it that you're good at everything? If you're a human being, you're allowed to be imperfect, you know.

Let's stop for today and hurry back.

Are you that excited about music class?

Yeah, I love it. The sound of the piano is exquisite!

Isn't it amazing that such a beautiful sound can come out of this piano?

You have so much energy. I'm wiped out from making the slippers.

Louis' favorite class was music. He could imagine the world he couldn't see with his eyes through the beautiful melodies of the piano.

Oh yeah. Today's the first day of reading class, isn't it?

TAP
TAP

Yeah!

I'll finally be freed from the torture!

Torture?

Yeah, do you know how hard it's been for me?

Every minute I get, I'm always asking someone to teach me how to read...

That's natural to be curious.

The more I ask, the more I want to know.

Anyway, I'm glad I can finally take this class that I've been dying to take!

Yeah, I was so excited I couldn't sleep last night.

I wish it was time for the class already!

At that time, books for the blind were made by embossing the letters on the paper so that the letters were raised above the paper and could be read by feeling it with one's finger.

This method was called "embossed printing."

This isn't what I was expecting. It takes too long to read a single word!

It was almost impossible to differentiate by touch alone between similarly shaped letters like 'Q' and 'O,' 'R' and 'B,' 'I' and 'T' and 'O' and 'C.'

Argh!

Some of the students got discouraged and gave up trying to read. However, Louis didn't stop moving his fingers until he could recognize and differentiate between each letter.

It wouldn't be me to quit now! I'm going to feel the letters a thousand times, a million times, until I can read them!

How's it going? Can you read pretty well now?

I can read it, but it takes so long to read one page.

And by the time I get to the end of the sentence, I can barely remember what was at the beginning of the sentence.

If the best student in the school is having such a hard time, how do you think I'm doing?

I want to be able to read without any obstacles, like a sighted person.

We don't have any choice though. This is the only way we can read.

There's gotta be another way.

Don't you think someone would've found it by now?

What?

In the past, they tried to make text for the blind with knots made of string, engraved sheets, and even stones. But none of them worked.

And the only method they could make books with was this embossed printing.

Really?

Anyway, I'm done reading this book. What should I read next?

Well, there's not much of a selection.

Why?

There are only fourteen books in the library.

One hundred forty?

No, fourteen!

No way! What kind of library only has fourteen books?

It requires a lot of money to make the books that we can read.

Since the letters are so big, the books have to be big and thick. They also have to be handmade.

That's why there aren't many books in the library.

Sigh. At this rate, the number of books for the blind is never going to increase.

From that day on, Louis thought of nothing else but how to make books for the blind easier to publish.

A new way...

Whenever he chatted with his friends, he would talk about books.

Do you guys have any ideas?

We've already told you several times, no!

How can these books be produced more easily?

STEP

STEP

Gabriel?

Hi, Louis. Are you thinking about books again?

Yeah. I still don't have any ideas.

Don't you think you're going a little crazy over this?

The other kids don't want to talk to you anymore. They're getting tired of talking about books.

Who cares? This is a very important problem! Can't you understand?

Once we can read, we won't have to live as beggars!

We won't have to work like animals doing hard labor!

05 Letters Made of Dots

The biggest issue is that the letters are so big that one page does not hold much content.

The letters need to be smaller.

But then we wouldn't be able to read them.

Around that time, Charles Barbier, an army captain who invented a nighttime writing system, came to visit the Institute for Blind Youth.

Is this the school for blind children?

How do they study if they're blind?

They can't see the books.

I heard they don't even have a decent writing system. I want to introduce them to my night writing.

Heh heh heh. If blind people use my writing system…

...then my night writing will become famous.

Is it true that you are here to teach our students a writing system?

Ah yes, that's right. Night writing will be a big help for the blind.

Night writing was created to send commands to soldiers at night. This system of using letters that can be read by touch was developed because the army needed to send messages to soldiers that they could read without a light.

Captain Barbier created a system of writing in which a sharp awl was used to punch holes or dots on thick paper. The night writing code consisted of a six-by-two grid of a total of twelve dots. Writing was done by punching holes and reading was done by feeling the raised dots.

Night writing is a system of writing with dots.

Dots?

Aha! Instead of writing letters the same way, they can be represented by something else.

If it's a simple symbol, it should be easy to distinguish with the fingertip.

How did this man think of this?

You punch holes like this.

Louis only thought of making the letters smaller and was therefore amazed when he learned that night writing used codes for each letter.

This is great! We can read this with just one finger, and we can read it accurately.

We can make books with night writing!

Let me try writing a sentence.

But Louis soon realized the fact that books could not be made with night writing code.

That's strange. Why can't I write a full sentence?

Why?

Because night writing was created for giving short military commands, it wasn't appropriate for writing full sentences.

Sigh. This isn't it either. I can write short words, but I can't connect the words to make sentences.

But that's a great idea to use dots to represent letters.

It'd be good if we could somehow adapt this system to be able to write sentences.

Ahhh, but who will create a writing system for us?

Should I give it a try?

No. If brilliant scholars couldn't do it, then how can I?

But not many books can be published with embossed printing...

Alright, let's do it. If no one's going to make it for us, I've got to do something!

92

Louis began researching ways to represent letters with dots. He grappled with it all day long and even in his sleep.

Some time later, the news spread to Captain Barbier.

What? He's trying to improve the dot system that I made? Does he know how much I put into this? And he thinks he can make it better?

Who is this Louis Braille? Have him sent to me!

94

I wasted my time on child's play.

It's not child's play. I'm very serious about this.

Oh really? Then explain to me the problems of my night writing!

What do you...

How dare you try to improve my invention and insult me like this!

Tell me what needs to be improved and how it needs to be improved! Right now!

First we have to standardize the way words are spelled.

That way, blind people will be able to read books.

Books? Why do people who can't even see in front of them need books? All you need are short notes or instructions!

I want to study. I want to learn much so that I can improve myself.

The blind studying!

No matter how much a blind person learns, it's impossible!

Anyway, is that all?

Yes.

Alright. You may go now.

Captain, would you be able to help…

I'll think about it.

Sigh. It doesn't look like I'll get any help from him.

He gave up hope on the captain, and began working on his own again.

PICK

PICK

PICK

When vacation came, Louis headed home. In his bag were tools for working on night writing.

Ah, the smell of home!

Louis, are you going out to work on your night code again?

Yup!

You don't rest for a minute.

I think I've almost got it. I can't stop working on it. I just know that once it's done, we'll be able to make books for the blind.

The village people laughed at Louis' antics. But he showed no interest in them and continued to silently work on the writing.

Louis took every chance he got to write with his stylus and paper.

Louis, when in the world do you sleep?

You were up almost all night last night!

When was the last time you ate?

Uh, well...

Take a break! Do you think the letters are going to suddenly form? You're going to become ill working like this!

Alright, alright. Thanks for looking out for me, sis. But really, it's almost complete. Just till then...

In actuality, he continued working on it for three whole years.

Arghhh!

I can't do it! I won't be able to do it! I can't do what nobody else has been able to do so far!

And I can't even see! How can I do something that even the accomplished captain couldn't do?

Huh? What's this?

100

The night writing code was based on sounds or phonemes. Unfortunately, the French language has a large number of phonemes.

Therefore, when the pronunciation of a word is complex, it can sometimes even require 100 dots to express the word.

It's a big mess of dots. I can't figure out what it's saying at all!

If we could represent the letters of the alphabet with dots, it'd be a lot easier…

Wait, the alphabet?

That's it! If we translate the letters of the alphabet into dots, we would only need 26 different arrangements! Hahaha! Why didn't I think of this earlier?

We can make a cell of six dots, instead of twelve.

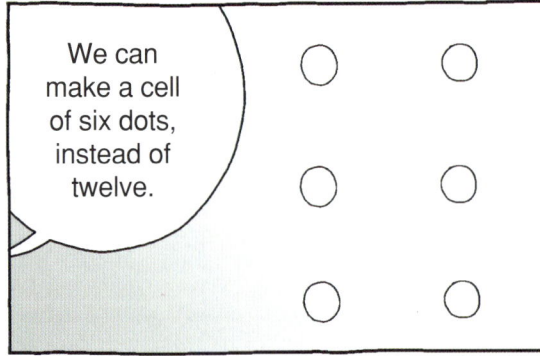

We assign a number to each dot.

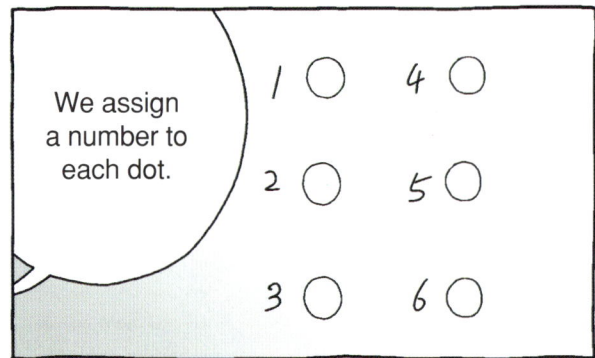

If there's a dot in the first space, then it's 'A.'

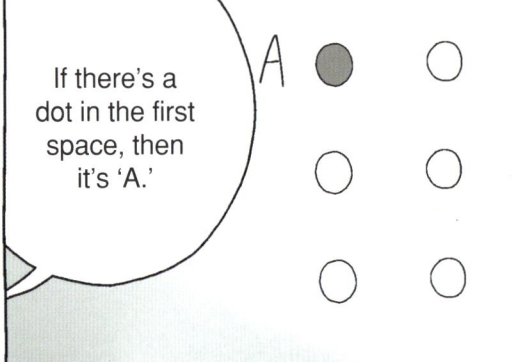

If there's a dot in the first and second space, then it's 'B.'

Yessss! It's done!

The dot alphabet that Louis made was quick and easy to read by touch, as well as write.

I've finally made the writing system!

Really?

That's great, son!

I gotta go and tell the kids at school!

Gabriel!

It's done! It's a system that we can use!

What? Are you serious?

Try it. It's a writing system made for us!

Wow, cool!

By representing the letters of the alphabet with six dots, it's easy to read.

If we use this, we can write fast, too. And afterwards, I can easily read what I wrote.

The dot alphabet was well-received by his classmates. The students at the school began to learn Louis' system.

Using this dot alphabet system, we can make books easily, too!

You're awesome!

Louis is the best!

Louis' dot alphabet spread throughout the school in no time.

106

Students would get together to learn and teach each other Louis' system of dots.

What are they doing? Something has been going on these days. Whenever there's a spare minute, students are gathering and whispering about something.

What are you kids doing here?

Oh, you haven't heard?

We're learning the dot alphabet.

Dot alphabet?

Louis made an alphabet system using dots. It's really easy to read and write.

What? Is that right?

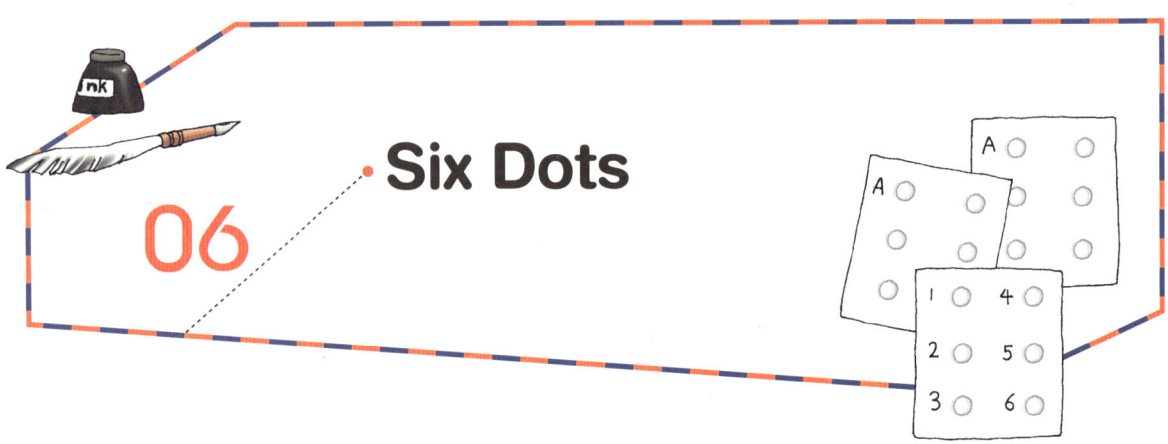

06 Six Dots

 Track 11 ▶

What is this dot alphabet? They said that you made it…

Principal's office

Alright. Go ahead and show me.

It's probably easier to understand if I demonstrate it for you.

Could you read me a passage from a book, any book?

Alright.

In the beginning, God created... the heavens... and the earth.

And on the sixth day, there was the evening and there was the morning.

Have you finished?

Now I'll read it back to you!

...

In the beginning, God created the heavens and the earth.

And on the sixth day, there was the evening and there was the morning.

That's amazing! You read it back verbatim. How old are you?

Fifteen, sir.

Unbelievable! A child, barely fifteen, who can't see, and is a student from our own school, has solved the problem that many scholars have been trying to solve for hundreds of years. I never would have imagined!

This is my chance! Let me ask the principal.

Sir, would it be possible to make a book using this dot system?

Do you mean a book for the blind?

Yes. I heard that the books that are currently made are too expensive and hard to read.

That is true.

My hope is that there can be many, many books...

...so that the blind can read and learn freely, just like the sighted.

You're right. There aren't enough books for the blind.

If there are more books, then the blind won't have to settle for a beggar's life.

So please, help me to publish a book using this dot alphabet!

I am put to shame. For such a young man, you have quite a vision! But...

Louis, you know that this is a charity school, right?

Yes.

Our school depends on the donations of its supporters. So unfortunately, we don't have extra funds to be able to publish a book.

Oh.

Then what if we write a letter to the patrons? And ask them to help us publish a book?

Could we explain how the dot alphabet works and how we can make books for the blind at a much lower cost?

Hmm.

Yes, let's do that! But don't expect too much.

Yes, sir. Thank you!

The principal began to write a letter to the school's supporters. He sent letters to aristocrats, the wealthy, and all those who had helped the blind in the past.

You're doing a wonderful job. It must be hard.

That is great news. However, these days, business has not been going well. I'm afraid I don't have the money.

Why not just keep things the way they are?

Unfortunately, the replies were all negative.

NO!!

Sigh. How can I tell Louis?

It's Louis, sir. I heard that you received another reply letter.

Come in.

Is it the same as the others?

I'm afraid so. I guess I don't have enough power or influence. I'm sorry.

We just want to have a decent life, but this society doesn't want to give us even this one small opportunity.

Why does the sighted population have such little interest in us?

...

I am not going to give up! Please send out more letters for us.

Alright, I promise.

Louis' dot alphabet began to slowly become known in the blind community. One day, the principal of another blind school came to visit.

Did you really make this dot alphabet?

Yes.

I can't believe it! It's amazing! A system so easy to use! If our students learned about this, they'd all want to learn and use this alphabet.

Sir, would you like to use this at your school?

Uh, well…

Our students are already using the dot system that I created. I can't abandon it!

This is just kid's play! Don't try to introduce this useless dot alphabet to people! Do you understand?

I have to go now.

Is my dot alphabet really not worth using?

It's a true treasure that is going to change the lives of the blind.

No, it's a great system.

That man was probably just jealous to see such a well-designed code.

I think I'll go back to my room now.

Go ahead.

...

Jealousy? I don't succumb to things like that. I'm not going to give up!

But the majority of the people who received the letter didn't outrightly say yes or no. They just acknowledged that they received the letter and asked for time to think about it.

The sighted people were too busy with their own lives that they had little time to think about the issue of the blind learning how to read.

Thank you for the letter you sent us.

Please give us some time to consider your proposal.

It's already been one year.

Fortunately, our school has implemented the dot alphabet into the curriculum, but that's only one hundred of us.

The blind community out there in the rest of the world probably can't read or write.

Even though I want to help them, I can't. I thought making the dot alphabet would solve everything.

Isn't there anything else I can do?

. . .

Louis!

Why haven't you been sending out letters these days? Have you already given up?

After all the effort I've put into this, nothing has changed.

That's not true. Nobody thought you'd actually be able to make the dot alphabet, but you did, didn't you? We're all working together with you to get the dot alphabet recognized.

As long as you don't give up, your work will be recognized one day. And there will come a day when every blind person will be using the dot alphabet that you made!

Thank you, sir. I won't give up.

Three years had passed, but there was still little interest in the dot alphabet. Louis had to put his regrets aside and move on.

During his school years, Louis earned top grades in all his subjects and won an award every year. The principal of the school was sad to have to send away his top student.

Have you thought about what you want to do after you graduate?

Well, I'm deciding between going back to my hometown or staying in Paris and earning money playing the piano.

What do you think about staying here at school and teaching the students?

I've never had such a bright student like you before. You would make a fine teacher!

As a teacher?

Actually, Louis wanted to stay in Paris. One of the reasons was that there were many people in the city who could help him promote the dot alphabet.

It didn't take long for Louis to decide. He decided to stay at the school and become a teacher.

Learning is fun, but teaching gives me a new kind of joy.

What should I teach tomorrow?

Okay, let's tell them about the French Revolution. I'd better write down my notes so I can remember the content of the lesson.

Louis was an excellent teacher. The students loved him.

Monsieur Braille, I don't understand.

Okay. Let's read this slowly, starting here.

Alright. That's it for today's class. See you all tomorrow.

Already?

Your class is too short!

We'll come visit your office. We want to hear the rest of the Bible story.

122

Louis, are you still practicing?

You practice the same songs every day. Don't you get bored?

What are you doing here?

I heard you're the official organist at church now.

The news spread all the way to Coupvray?

I'm flattered.

Let's see how much you've improved.

Just name a song.

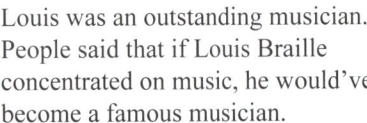

Louis was an outstanding musician. People said that if Louis Braille concentrated on music, he would've become a famous musician.

Louis loved music, too, but he loved the dot alphabet more. In order to introduce others to the music that he loved, he worked on a way to translate music and numbers into dots as well.

Now even the music score? Why don't you take it easy?

Sigh. I still have a long way to go.

Around that time, Louis began to write a book himself using the dot alphabet. The completed book was added to the school library collection.

I'd better stop for today. My shoulder hurts too much.

I want to make many more books, but the 24-hour day is too short.

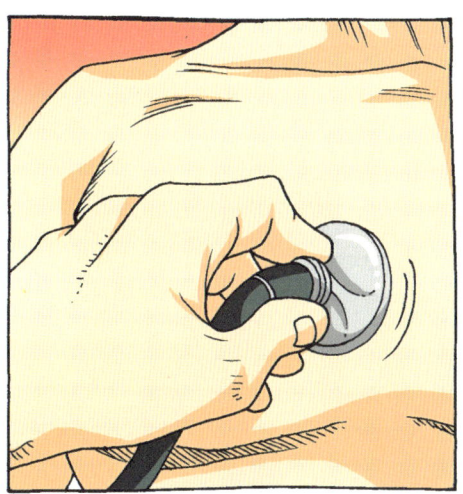

It's alright. Please tell us what it is.

I'm sure you already know this but…

It's my lungs, isn't it?

Yes, it's tuberculosis.

I see. I suspected as much.

Are you in your right mind? He said you have tuberculosis!

It's okay. If I go back to my hometown where the air is clean and get a lot of rest, it'll get better.

Yes, you need to get plenty of rest.

In those days, tuberculosis was a serious, life-threatening disease. Both Louis and the doctor knew that he would not be able to completely recover from the disease.

I'd better go now. Get some rest.

Yeah, thanks.

...

I'm only twenty-six...

I can't go yet. What will happen to the dot alphabet if I die?

Louis Braille had not once given up so far. He stood up and fought when he first became blind and when he created the dot alphabet system.

I am not going to just wait for death!

127

07 · Hope for the Blind

 CD2 Track 21 ▶

While Braille was resting in his hometown, he received some good news.

Principal Pignier!

You've waited a long time for this. We now have enough money to make a book about the dot alphabet.

Thank you, sir.

Not at all. It's my pleasure to be able to take part in this great invention.

The two of them began to put together the book that would introduce the dot alphabet. They put much time and effort into making this book better than any existing book on this subject. They entitled the book, *Method of Writing Words, Music and Plainsong by Means of Dots for Use by the Blind and Arranged for Them.*

I think the title is too long.

No, it captures the whole content of this book. It's a great title.

Now a lot more people will probably become interested in the dot alphabet.

Let's first send copies of this book to our school patrons and well-known members of society!

Yes, sir.

Sir, is it true?

SLAM

I'm afraid so. I sent the books with a letter, but they were all sent back.

N-no...

Braille directly met with noblemen in order to tell them about the dot alphabet.

Please take a look at this book.

It explains the dot alphabet which can be used to make books for the blind.

Why do the blind need books?

In order to improve the standard of living for the blind. If we can study, we can also become lawyers or scientists some day.

Scientist?

Lawyer?

131

Braille was now thirty years old, an age people usually consider young. However, there was not much time left for Braille.

Then something worse happened to him.

Are you really quitting?

I'm sorry. It's what I have to do.

And I wasn't able to help you get the dot alphabet recognized...

Braille lost Principal Pignier —his teacher, his coworker whom he struggled with, and his most loyal friend.

The new principal, Armand Dufau, did not like taking risks so he did not particularly like Braille's alphabet.

The blind using a different alphabet than everyone else? If that's the case, then they'll just become even more ostracized!

I can't stop the use of the dot alphabet here at school while Braille is still here.

But as soon as I get a chance, I'm going to put a stop to it!

!

Around that time, Braille's illness got worse so he followed his doctor's advice to go back to his hometown and get some rest.

Finally, Monsieur Braille has left.

We have to take this chance to stop the use of the dot alphabet.

Right! To have to learn this unnecessary new alphabet...

It's a nuisance!

All of the students are using his dot alphabet so we can't just go back to the way we used to teach our classes.

To have to learn a whole new system…

We have a lot of work already without having to learn the dot alphabet.

Moreover, there's a reason why the dot alphabet cannot be made widely known to the rest of the world.

If all the books start to be published with the dot system, then sighted people like us won't be able to work at schools for the blind anymore.

Even now, isn't Louis Braille more popular with the students than us?

Now that you mention it, this is a big problem. We've got to do away with the dot alphabet at once.

Let's take this opportunity to burn all the dot alphabet books!

Hmmm, everyone feels the same way.

From now on, there will be no more use of the dot alphabet. If you're caught using it, be warned that there will be a punishment.

136

I learned how to read because of the dot alphabet.

Me too. I don't want to go back to being jealous of my younger brothers because they can read.

Then what should we do?

We've got to let people know far and wide about this alphabet.

And let's teach it to the freshmen who haven't learned it yet.

Meanwhile, Braille had spent much time at home slowly recovering and prepared to return to school.

Isn't that Braille?

When did he come back?

Something is strange.

137

139

After his conversation with Principal Dufau, Braille became perplexed. Braille began to waver in the ideas he had firmly believed in.

Have I been wrong in my thinking?

Oh no! The principal has taken all of Monsieur Braille's books!

What's going on?

Principal Dufau said that he's going to burn all your books.

What?

Give it to me!

You can't! These books are the future of the blind!

Please don't burn the books!

Quiet! Go back to your classrooms!

The blind don't need this many books. The fourteen books in the library are enough!

Ack!

140

They will only have empty dreams after being able to read books. Dreams that will never happen!

Quickly, set these books on fire!

Yes, sir.

Hey!

No, my books!

Sir, don't get so close to the fire. It's hot!

Let go of me! I have to save my books!

Monsieur Braille, what do we do?

141

Louis Braille felt like he was falling back into a dark pit of despair. He had gone through many trials before, but this time, he could not endure it. He had invested his whole life into the dot alphabet, and now it was being taken away from him. He fell into deeper despair each day.

How could this happen? It must be a nightmare...

143

They can take our dot stylus away, but that won't stop us.

We can use these knitting needles to write the dot alphabet!

Hahaha. I took a knitting needle, too!

Tsk, tsk. They say if you're not smart, then your body will suffer for it.

What?

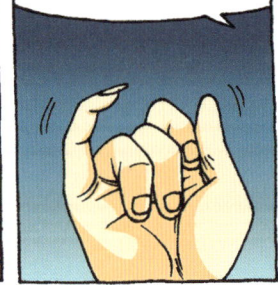

If you grow out your fingernail like this and file it sharp, you can punch dots with it!

The kid with bad grades sure has the best tricks.

Hmph, see if you can do better!

146

Really?

Yes. After learning the dot alphabet, I was able to write a daily journal for the first time.

And it's great to be able to take notes during class to remember what we learned!

How can we throw away such a useful system?

We're going to keep using it no matter how much they punish us!

That's right. I made the dot alphabet system for kids like these! If they burned my books, I'll just make them again! I'll talk to the principal once more.

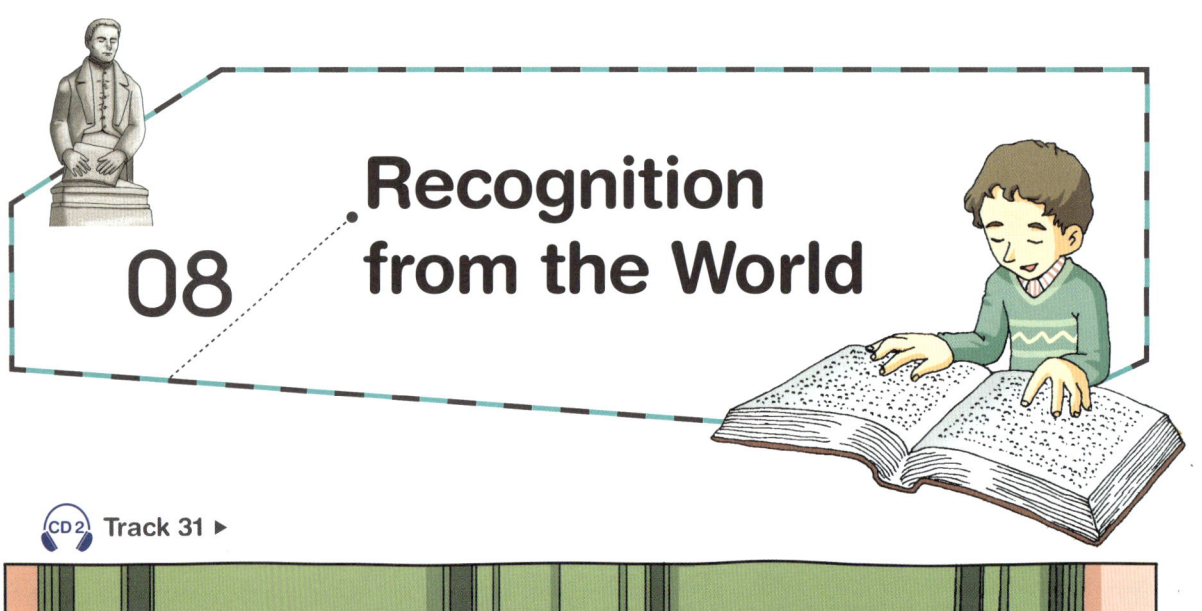

08 Recognition from the World

CD 2 Track 31 ▶

I've already said no!

I am certain that the students need this!

These children, more than anyone else, want to be able to see the world around them through literacy!

What school doesn't listen to the opinion of its students?

I am the one with the authority! My word is the law at this school.

Encouraged by the students, Braille decided to stand up once again to fight for the dot system. In addition, another person began to strongly advocate the dot alphabet, a fellow teacher at the school named Joseph Guadet. He observed the students carefully and examined the dot alphabet system closely.

This is revolutionary!

The dot alphabet cannot just remain here. It must be used by blind people all around the world.

Principal Dufau, this has to be widely promoted!

What are you talking about?

You may be able to stop our students from using the dot alphabet for now.

But you won't be able to stop the blind community around the world from using it.

The blind community around the world?

This is an amazing system. Without a doubt, it will spread far and wide.

But what will people think if they hear that the school where the dot alphabet was invented had banned its use?

This dot alphabet is going to change the lives of the blind!

Is it really that great? I suppose that's why the students are refusing to give it up.

If this writing system becomes widely known, then people around the world will hear about you as well, Principal Dufau.

Hum.

They'll hear about me? I like the sound of that!

Alright. Let's recall the ban on the dot alphabet.

Around this time, Principal Dufau put much effort into relocating the school. The current building was too worn down and falling apart.

The new school building was soon completed. For the opening ceremony of the new building, Principal Dufau made a dramatic decision.

Let's introduce the dot alphabet at the opening ceremony.

Huh? Why the sudden change of heart?

Well, since you have a strong conviction about it, and the students seem to favor it as well...

With the introduction of the dot alphabet, in addition to the construction of the school's new building, I will be sure to get much recognition.

On February 22, 1844, it was a particularly fine day. Braille could hardly sleep the night before.

Today is the day.

All of the important dignitaries are here. This is indeed a history-making moment!

Mother, Louis is sitting over there!

Oh, I'm so proud of him!

How long have I waited for this moment!

Joseph Guadet walked up to the platform with a book in his hand.

I would like to present to you about a writing system for the blind, called the dot alphabet.

Dot alphabet? What's that?

I've never heard of it. Have you?

Well, I haven't, either.

By arranging six dots in different arrangements, the 26 letters of the alphabet can be encoded.

Now, Principal Dufau will demonstrate how the dot alphabet is used.

I will read a passage from a book and this student will write it all down.

Then she will give what she has written to a student who is waiting outside the hall. And he will read it back to us.

She has used the dot alphabet to write on this paper.

Long ago in a village...

It's a trick!

He memorized it before he came in here!

It's not a trick!

Please calm down. Let's demonstrate it once more. If anyone in the audience has something they can read, please stand up.

I have an old book with me. I'll read it!

The blind student listened to the passage from the man's book and wrote it down using the dot alphabet.

Then the other student came in and read what the boy had written. The audience exploded with cheers at this unbelievable feat.

The blind will finally be able to read as much as they want!

The presentation was a success. Braille shed tears of joy in the midst of the people's cheers. It made up for all his past sufferings.

The difficult struggle to promote the dot alphabet finally came to a close. However, Braille's health continued to worsen.

Whew. I don't know if it's from all of the excitement, but my body feels weaker.

In the end, Braille could no longer continue teaching.

I can't teach anymore but I won't stop making books.

You've just started recovering and you're already at the books again?

Take it easy.

I'll be okay.

Louis, I finished making this book!

Good job. Then here's another one for you to do.

Some of the teachers from our school are going to go to another school for the blind and teach the dot alphabet there. People are also calling the dot alphabet "Braille."

They're calling it Braille?

Yes.

Braille!

Wow...

It doesn't seem real.

You're finally getting the recognition you deserve!

With all this good news, my life can come to an end and I'll have no regrets!

What are you talking about? You have to live much longer so that you can receive all the honor that's coming your way!

I'm satisfied with the fact that we can have the opportunity to have a better life.

I don't want wealth and fame.

No. This is an incredible accomplishment.

Soon afterwards, Braille's condition continued to worsen to the point where he was bedridden.

I don't have much time left.

But I've got to finish this book first.

160

Even in the midst of illness, he never stopped working.

COUGH

COUGH

Whew.
Finished one more volume...

Each book that gets made will improve the life of the blind just a little bit more.

Tonight's rain sounds particularly gloomy.

Gotta start the next volume.

But I feel so weak today...

Ahh!

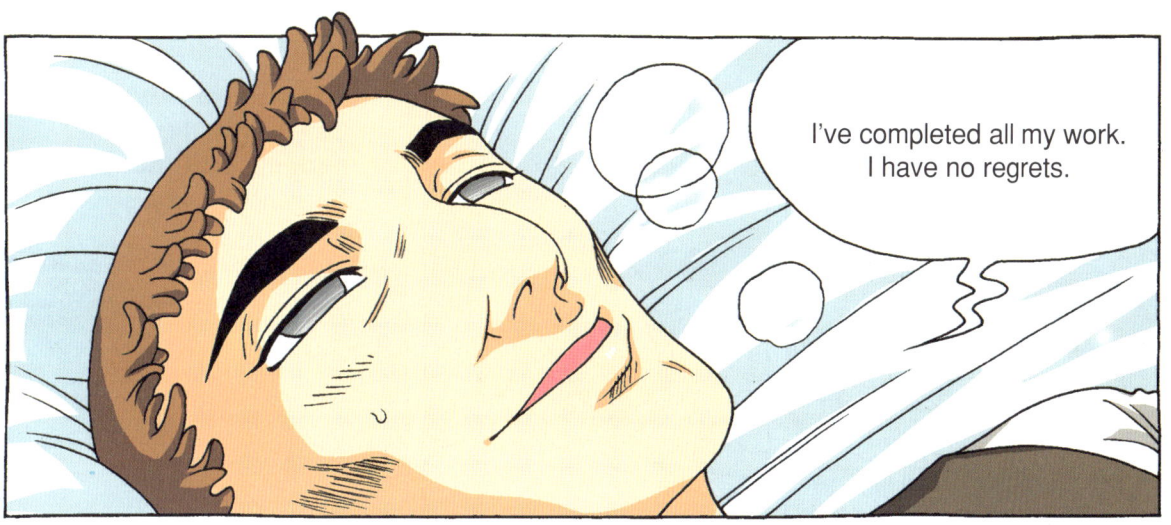

I've completed all my work. I have no regrets.

My dots are going to one day be able to change the life of the blind.

Mary, I brought a present for you!

A present?

Here!

Is it a book?

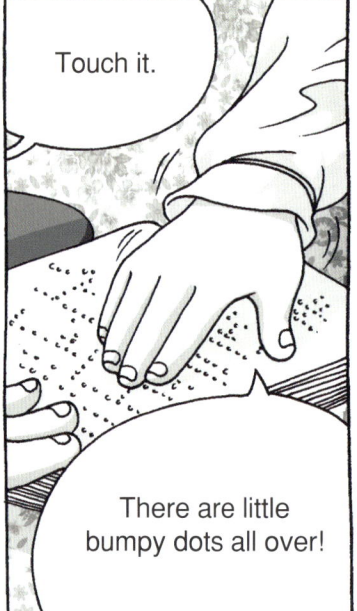

164

Braille's life ended quietly.
Only a few of his closest friends
and his family members came to
his small grave.

Braille's death was not covered in any
newspaper in France. He left a great legacy
but no one seemed to notice his passing.

However, 100 years after his death, in 1952, every newspaper around the world featured Louis Braille. The achievement of the Braille system was not recognized during Braille's lifetime but it received people's attention 100 years later.

Louis Braille's body, which had been resting in his hometown village, was exhumed and relocated to the Pantheon National Cemetery, which is reserved for honored citizens. His funeral procession included the president of France and other distinguished people. Also in the procession were hundreds of blind people who wanted to pay tribute to Braille.

There is a town square in Coupvray, France, Braille's hometown, which is named after him. Inscribed there are the words, "Louis Braille opened the doors of knowledge to all those who cannot see." He gave eyes to those who cannot see. Through the Braille system, the blind no longer had to merely thirst for knowledge...

They were able to dream of becoming a scientist, a novelist, a lawyer, whatever they wanted to become. Louis Braille enabled those who cannot see to break out of their darkness, dream of a bright future, and have the power of choice. He will forever be remembered in the hearts of not only the blind but of the whole world.

LOUIS BRAILLE

1809 – 1852

CREADOR DEL SISTEMA
DE LECTURA YESCRITORA
AARA CIEGOS

Word Search

● Find the words which are hidden horizontally, vertically and diagonally.

```
Q M Z G Q M Z G Q M Z G Q Q M Z G Q M T
W S I N V E N T I O N H W W N A H W N O
E B Q J A B Q J E T B A R B A R I O B M
R V C K R D C K R V C K R R V C K P V M
E C W O R S E N T C D L T T C D U P C E
V X E Q Y X E O Y X E Q Y Y X E N O X M
E Z V W U D V W C Z V W R U Z V J R Z W
A N A E I A E T I A R E E I A R A T A I
L S I R O S G C O S T R C O S G S U S T
P D C G P D H T O D H E O P D H T N D A
A P A Y H F U Y A T U Y V A F U Y I F D
S E S U S T I N C R I G E I N G U T G R
D R S I D H M I D H O I R D H O I Y H A
F M A B S O R A F J T J F F J T J F J W
G I N Q G K R E R E P I E N T S B G K C
H S A N H L E N H E E N H H L E N H L E
J S T M J Q T A U T D O R I T Y M J B T
L I E Q L W Y Q L W Y Q L L W Y Q L U Y
Z O K F Z W K F Z W K F Z Z S U F T R R
X N M E X P R I N C I P A L E M U X N M
C R Q G C R Q C P C I G H T R Q C U R Q
```

| invention | opportunity | principal | nightmare |
| burn | worsen | recover | permission |

Vocabulary

● Match each word to the correct meaning.

1. knowledge	• 눈이 먼
2. blind	• 거지
3. sight	• 지식
4. beggar	• 출판하다
5. publish	• 교육
6. dot	• 가능한
7. give up	• 운명
8. destiny	• 포기하다
9. possible	• 시력
10. tuberculosis	• 결핵
11. education	• 만들다
12. create	• 점

Guess What?

● Guess what he said in the blank.

It's Louis, sir. I heard that you received another reply letter.

Come in.

Is it the same as the others?

I'm afraid so. I guess I don't have enough power or influence. I'm sorry.

We just want to have a decent life, but this society doesn't want to give us even this one small opportunity.

Why does the sighted population have such little interest in us?

...

Alright, I promise.

Quizzes

● Choose the best answers for the blanks.

1. Louis Braille was born in _____.

   a. England   b. France   c. Spain

2. Braille letters are made up of _____.

   a. dots   b. lines   c. holes

3. When he was three, he had an accident with an _____ injuring his left eye.

   a. anchor   b. ink   c. awl

4. The Braille system used _____ dots to read.

   a. raised   b. deepened   c. underlined

5. Louis Braille attended a special school for the _____.

   a. deaf   b. blind   c. crippled

6. Louis Braille was excellent at the school, so he received a _____.

   a. scholarship   b. allowance   c. punishment

7. By 1824, 15-year-old Louis had found 63 ways to use a _____ cell.

   a. five-dots   b. six-dots   c. seven-dots

8. He spent his life _____ the system to as many people as possible.

   a. showing   b. sending   c. teaching

9. Braille helps blind people _____.

   a. dance   b. read   c. speak

10. Today he is celebrated as a _____ for all blind people.

   a. principal   b. brother   c. hero

Answers : 1-b, 2-a, 3-c, 4-a, 5-b, 6-a, 7-b, 8-c, 9-b, 10-c

Braille Chart

a   b   c   d   e   f   g   h   i   j

k   l   m   n   o   p   q   r   s   t

u   v   w   x   y   z

,   ;   :   .   ?   !   "   (*   )

apostrophe   -   /

1   2   3   4   5   6   7   8   9   0

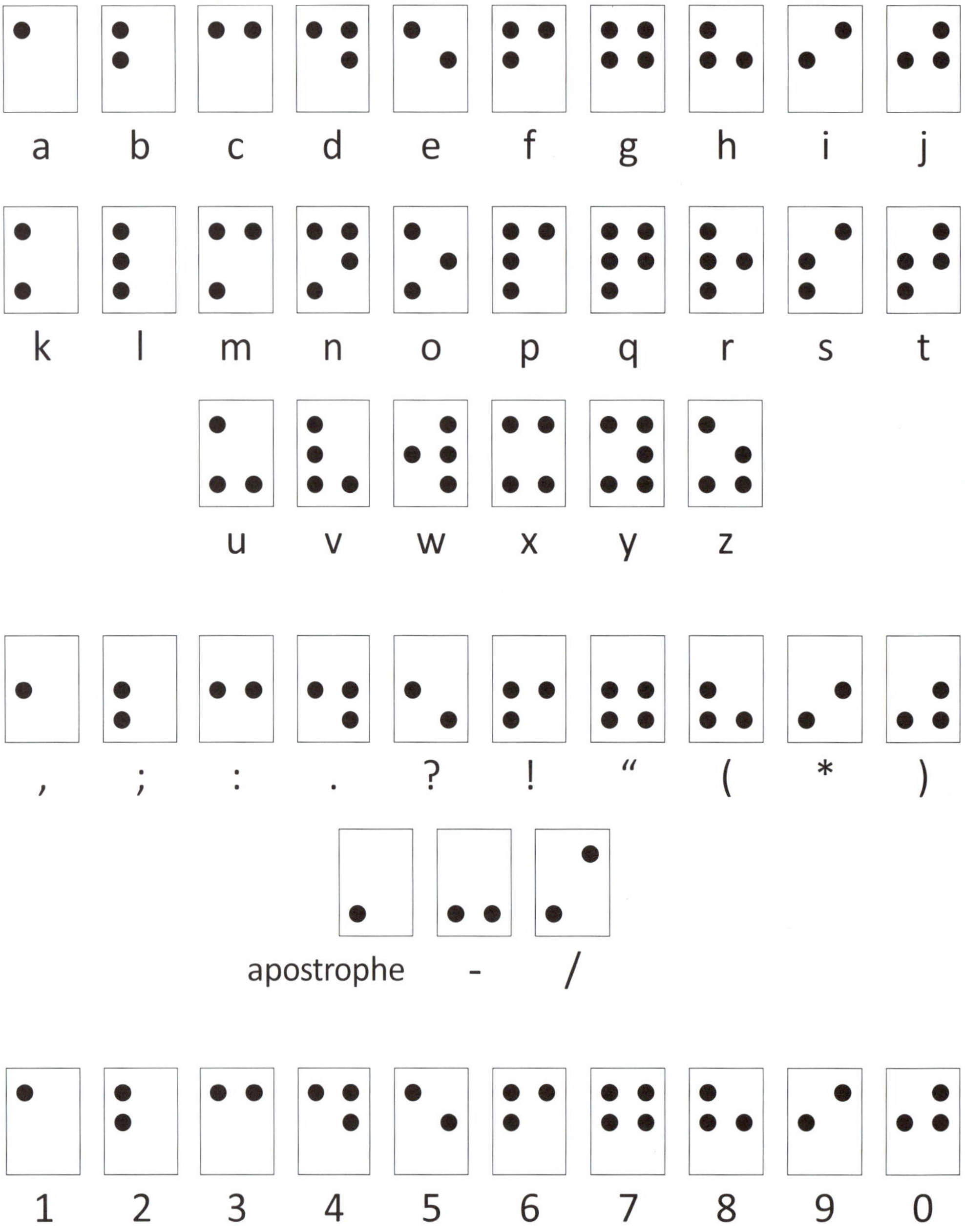

Let's Read Braille

● Use the Braille table to decode the following words. Write your answers in the boxes underneath.

점자를 찍는 모습

시각 장애인용 점자 시계

1.

2.

3.

4.

5.

6.

★Write your name in Braille. _____

연표

1809년 　　　 1월 4일, 프랑스 쿠브레이에서 태어났습니다.

1812년 　3세 아버지의 작업장에서 실수로 왼쪽 눈을 다칩니다.

1819년 　10세 파리에 있는 왕립 맹아 학교에 들어갑니다.

1821년 　12세 샤를 바르비에 대위로부터 야간 문자를 배웁니다.

1824년 　15세 점 여섯 개로 알파벳 26개를 표시할 수 있는 점자를 만들어 냅니다.

1825년 　16세 점자를 찍을 수 있는 점자판을 만듭니다.

1826년 　17세 왕립 맹아 학교를 졸업하고 모교에서 보조 교사가 됩니다.

1827년 　18세 점자 알파벳을 이용하여 책을 만듭니다.
　　　　　　　 수학 기호와 음악 기호를 표현할 수 있는 점자를 만듭니다.

1828년 　19세 모교에서 정식 교사가 되어 음악, 지리, 수학, 문법을 가르칩니다.

1833년 　24세 성 니콜라스 데 샹 성당의 오르간 연주자가 됩니다.

1834년 25세 점자 알파벳에 '브라유'라는 이름이 붙습니다.

1835년 26세 결핵에 걸려 건강이 매우 나빠졌습니다.

1841년 32세 피네 교장 선생님이 학교를 떠나고 뒤포 교장 선생님이 옵니다.
             병이 점점 심해져 고향으로 요양을 떠납니다.

1844년 35세 국립 맹아 학교 신축 건물   점자를 알립니다.
             병 때문에 몸이 약해져서 교사를 그만둡니다.

1847년 38세 브라유 문자 인쇄기가 최초로 만들어집니다.

1851년 42세 감기에 걸립니다.

1852년 43세 1월 6일, 파리에서 세상을 떠납니다.

1868년   점자 알파벳이 맹인들을 위한 공식 문자로 인정됩니다.

1952년   시신이 프랑스의 국립묘지 판테온으로 옮겨집니다.

who? 01	Barack Obama	979-11-5639-023-7
who? 02	Charles Darwin	979-11-5639-024-4
who? 03	Bill Gates	979-11-5639-025-1
who? 04	Hillary Clinton	979-11-5639-026-8
who? 05	Stephen Hawking	979-11-5639-027-5
who? 06	Oprah Winfrey	979-11-5639-028-2
who? 07	Steven Spielberg	979-11-5639-029-9
who? 08	Thomas Edison	979-11-5639-030-5
who? 09	Abraham Lincoln	979-11-5639-031-2
who? 10	Martin Luther King, Jr.	979-11-5639-032-9
who? 11	Louis Braille	979-11-5639-033-6
who? 12	Albert Einstein	979-11-5639-034-3
who? 13	Jane Goodall	979-11-5639-035-0
who? 14	Walt Disney	979-11-5639-036-7
who? 15	Winston Churchill	979-11-5639-037-4
who? 16	Warren Buffett	979-11-5639-008-4
who? 17	Nelson Mandela	979-11-5639-009-1
who? 18	Steve Jobs	979-11-5639-010-7
who? 19	J. K. Rowling	979-11-5639-011-4
who? 20	Jean-Henri Fabre	979-11-5639-012-1
who? 21	Vincent van Gogh	979-11-5639-013-8
who? 22	Marie Curie	979-11-5639-014-5
who? 23	Henry David Thoreau	979-11-5639-015-2
who? 24	Andrew Carnegie	979-11-5639-016-9
who? 25	Coco Chanel	979-11-5639-017-6
who? 26	Charlie Chaplin	979-11-5639-018-3
who? 27	Ho Chi Minh	979-11-5639-019-0
who? 28	Ludwig van Beethoven	979-11-5639-020-6
who? 29	Mao Zedong	979-11-5639-021-3
who? 30	Kim Dae-jung	979-11-5639-022-0